RICHARD MISHAAN
DESIGN ARCHITECTURE AND INTERIORS

RICHARD MISHAAN
DESIGN
ARCHITECTURE AND INTERIORS

RICHARD MISHAAN

with

Jacqueline Terrebonne

VENDOME
NEW YORK · LONDON

CONTENTS

DESIGN HAS BEEN A PART OF MY LIFE FOR AS LONG AS I CAN REMEMBER—and perhaps even earlier. I was born in Bogotá, Colombia. During my childhood, my family lived in a house that had been designed by a protégé of Frank Lloyd Wright in 1956. It was a flat-roofed, Prairie-style home with multiple split-level rooms, frameless windows, minimal moldings, a reflection pool, and a stone feature wall. The library was furnished with pieces by Edward Wormley for Dunbar and other notable mid-century designers. The décor of the living room was entirely different: eighteenth-century tables, étagères, and decorative arts mixed with modern pieces. Even at a young age, the eclectic combination struck me as perfectly balanced and harmonious.

My maternal grandmother's home, where my mother grew up, was just the opposite. Later in life, I realized she must have been inspired by a visit to Château de Chenonceau. The interior architecture was quite classical, with limestone-clad walls on the first floor and generous moldings throughout. Not everything was French though. Shortly after World War II ended, she discovered that her sister and her mother had survived German war camps and that the king of Denmark had taken them in and made them citizens. From then on, my grandmother visited Denmark

INTRODUCTION

often and became enamored with the Scandinavian modernists, who were fast gaining in popularity. She replaced a chandelier with a lighting fixture by Paavo Tynell and layered the home with pieces by Hans Wegner, Finn Juhl, and Poul Kjaerholm. The result was fresh and unique—a true reflection of her personal taste and style.

Both women collected art and prided themselves on finding interesting emerging artists. My grandmother was drawn to Impressionist works, and my mother gravitated toward Latin American artists and other contemporary artists from around the world. The fact that all these disparate elements coexisted in each home helped me appreciate the power of the strong mix early on and even sparked my desire to study architecture and design. Today, my homes are a tapestry of all these things. Many have been handed down to me; others I've found on my extensive travels or even just walking around my neighborhood. As a result of these multiple layers of influence, eclecticism and maximalism are what I find comfortable, warm, and cozy. They remind me of home. They are home.

As an interior designer, I strive to create that same feeling of comfort for my clients. I use my appreciation and knowledge of the arts, architecture, and design to

help them identify their own personal style. In the process, they often discover their passion for it. Early in my career, after spending five years traveling the world to source artisanal furniture and decorative arts for clients, I opened my own shop, Homer, on Madison Avenue in 1997. Before my trip, I asked a friend, Christiane Celle—a visionary in all she does—who she considered to be up and coming in home design. She told me to look up her friend Olivier Gagnère when I was in Paris. He had recently designed the Café Marly at the Louvre and truly had his finger on the pulse. He invited me to an exhibition he had participated in that was a design version of a *cadavre exquis*, or "exquisite corpse," which is a collective work begun by one artist and sequentially added to by other artists. Gagnère and his circle had applied the concept to furniture, rugs, and lighting. The group—all newcomers—included Hervé Van der Straeten, Olivier Lesage, Thomas Boog, and Christophe Delcourt. I went on to represent all of them in my shop and held shows for each one. Homer became the go-to destination for the design world for the next sixteen years. Although the shop has long since closed, my belief in the power that unique design pieces bring to an interior has never been stronger. I'm always on the hunt for the next great artisan or the undiscovered piece of collectible design that will become the catalyst for an entire interior.

In addition to collectible design, my passion for fine art drives my entire creative process. Throughout my career, I've had the good fortune to work with incredible collectors on their homes. My job is to create a context for their extraordinary artworks and show them off to best visual effect. I often use trips to museums to spark new ideas for this. When I stop by the Metropolitan or MoMA or any of hundreds of museums around the globe, I'm not looking for art to buy. Instead, I'm informing my eye and taking in details such as how a piece is hung and lit or the fascinating color combinations in a period room. As I study the works and their settings, design ideas bubble up. A visit to a David Hockney exhibition at the Royal Academy of Arts once changed my entire direction on a project.

You can see the way my design process unfolds in the mood boards that open each chapter in this book. These images, rich with detail and inspiration, define what I'm trying to achieve with each project. For me, the mood board is where every project begins and ends: it sets the direction from the start and represents the cohesive thinking behind all the elements that make up the whole of the completed job. Whereas my previous books, *Modern Luxury* (2009) and *Artfully Modern* (2014), featured only residential interiors, I've broken the mold in this monograph. In addition to residential interiors in country and seaside homes, as well

as city apartments, I've included hotels, a restaurant, and show houses, which are my laboratories for experimenting with new design concepts. Taken together, they demonstrate the full range of the Richard Mishaan Design portfolio and show how I work within the constraints of budgets and space. Throughout, I pull back the curtain on my creative process to reveal how I achieve the end results.

My whole married life I've joked that my wife, Marcia, is the science channel and I'm the arts and entertainment network. I truly love all the art forms, but my favorites are the visual and performing arts. The sets of operas and ballets can inspire a million design ideas. Can you imagine constructing an entire Italian village to last just one night as they do for *Tosca*? When I work in my office on the weekends, I often blast not only operas but also jazz, contemporary music, and Broadway musicals, especially those of Stephen Sondheim. His songs, filled with their inimitable romantic cynicism, have been the soundtrack of countless moments in my life. But more than any other musical, the Pulitzer Prize–winning *Sunday in the Park with George*, about the life of famed Pointillist Georges Seurat, stirs something deep within me. From the opening

number, my heart soars. George says the words that to me are the secret recipe for creativity: "Composition, Balance, Light, and Harmony." It's what I set out to accomplish in every space I create. My artist friends and I have discussed how inspiration is not at everyone's fingertips but must be searched for externally and internally by digging deep inside. I've had to do it time and again for clients because I want every project to be distinct and unique. The way George breaks down the elements of creativity on stage, that's how I approach every project in the book. And just as Sondheim's words have guided me, I hope the work on the following pages guides you in your search for—and understanding of—creativity and beauty in the world.

PAGE 13: The library in the home of my maternal grandmother, Mrs. DeGutt.

OPPOSITE, FROM LEFT TO RIGHT: My fashionable parents; my maternal grandmother, her daughter (my mom), and her sister in Denmark; me in my parents' home, decorated with Gabriella Crespi and Karl Springer furniture.

ABOVE LEFT AND RIGHT: The classically French architecture of my maternal grandmother's home, seen in the stairway's upper gallery (left) and living room (right).

COUNTRY & SEASIDE

DESIGNING AROUND A FABULOUS ART COLLECTION ALWAYS MAKES FOR AN interesting project, but what's even more exciting is working with artists on their own home. When friends of mine, painter John Alexander and ceramist Fiona Waterstreet, asked me to assist them with their 400-year-old barn in Amagansett, New York, I jumped at the opportunity. They both have incredible minds and strong visual inclinations; the challenge for me was that each of them had a completely different vision of the overall direction. He didn't want anything fancy, preferring that nonchalant, thrown-together look so many painters have historically embraced. As for her, the fancier the better. It was up to me to unite these opposing sensibilities into a harmonious yet uncompromising middle ground.

Having worked with them on their city apartment, I had navigated these waters before and used that experience to tap into their kindred bohemian spirits. The historic structure presented the perfect envelope for marrying their tastes. We opted to leave nods to the building's original use intact, keeping it uninsulated to preserve the texture of the walls and retaining its sliding wood doors. The main living area is a soaring, loft-like space, with the dining area differentiated only by a step up. The

ARTISTS IN RESIDENCE

bedroom upstairs opens to the floor below, so we added screens to ensure a level of privacy and hung giant curtains for softness.

As artists, they're not into frilly nonsense, but Fiona did want some luxurious fabrics and interesting furniture to elevate the look. I came up with the idea of covering rich velvet upholstery with informal linen slipcovers in the summer. Accent fabrics merge their wish lists. She loves chintz. He wanted animal prints. For every item that's toned down, there's a counterpoint that's quite the opposite. Even the dining chairs have a similar duality—I covered the backs with a sumptuously patterned fabric but chose a plainer, more durable fabric for the seats.

In the media room we embraced the past—combining comfortable English furniture, including a George Smith sofa, with rakes and other farm equipment casually placed around the room. Overhead, a chandelier is strung on a rope, so it can be lowered to light the candles. We left the stucco walls the way they were, and they add so much character even if it means portable heaters are necessary in the winter.

John's paintings animate all rooms of the house—bringing life, beauty, and personality. However, none of the decoration is built around these works as a focal

point, as artworks are sold and move on to other homes. But one work of art will always stay, and that is the garden, which John has meticulously and painstakingly created, planted, and cared for. It closely resembles Claude Monet's garden at Giverny, and spending time in it makes you feel like you're inside one of his *Water Lilies* canvases. We carefully placed and designed outdoor rooms with rattan furniture and an enchanting pergola to make the most of these awe-inspiring vistas.

The house is filled with beautiful things and yet, with art coming and going, it is constantly changing. Overall, the place is comfy and cozy and presents the perfect example of understanding how to make the best life for yourself in a setting that truly reflects who you are without subscribing to trends—and how real elegance shines when it's understated.

PAGE 19 AND OPPOSITE: Mood boards express the artful mix found in a Hamptons retreat.

PAGES 22-23: This lush, painterly landscape was inspired by Claude Monet's garden at Giverny.

LEFT: In the entry, the feeling of rustic charm is established with sliding barn doors and brick floors.

PAGE 26: Works by the homeowners are on display throughout the house, including ceramics by Fiona Waterstreet and paintings by John Alexander.

PAGE 27: In the dining area of the main, loft-like living space, the combination of fabrics on the chairs expresses her desire for fancy and his for something more casual.

PAGES 28-29: The 400-year-old barn's uninsulated walls create the perfect backdrop for a mix of patterned fabrics, antiques, and art.

PAGE 30: Below a work by Alexander, a chair and pillow combine her request for chintz and his preference for animal prints.

PAGE 31: A cozy nook is enlivened with an array of patterned pillows and a work by Peter Beard.

RIGHT: In the media room, farm equipment and oversized baskets recall the barn's original, functioning past.

PAGE 34: In Waterstreet's office, the texture of roughhewn wood slats plays off the woven seat of an antique chair.

PAGE 35: The homes of artists provide backdrops for endless combinations of artworks and interesting objects.

PAGES 36-37: The primary bedroom is separated from the main living area below by a simple partition yet feels private owing to the intimate furniture plan and personal objects.

PAGE 38: A certain artistry exists in a bath this simple.

PAGE 39: A painting by Alexander surmounts a sofa upholstered in a bold Pierre Frey print.

LEFT: The guest bedroom is clearly an addition to the house, retaining the shingles of the original exterior wall.

PAGE 42: Outside the kitchen, a console is used for displaying plants or laying out a summer buffet.

PAGE 43: An antique farm table serves as the kitchen island.

PAGE 44: The exquisite garden functions as the house's most spectacular room.

PAGE 45: Every chair is the best seat in the house under a vine-covered pergola.

THERE'S SOMETHING SO EXCITING ABOUT WORKING WITH CLIENTS ON multiple homes. Over time, you get to watch as their aesthetic evolves, but I enjoy it even more when the projects are in different locations. Recasting their sensibility from city to country or beach to mountain is such an interesting exercise in design, and I embrace every aspect of it. In this case, close friends whom I had worked with on two city residences bought a horse farm in rural Westchester County, New York. They wanted a place away from the city where they could spend quiet family time as well as entertain guests in relaxed surroundings while pursuing their passion for horseback riding.

As you approach the house, old trees arch over the meandering drive. Horses graze in the meadow. It's sheer pastoral bliss, and I wanted the interiors to live up to that feeling in anything but a clichéd way. Dating to 1870, the house had beautiful bones, which I thought were important to maintain when updating the floor plan to make it livable for a modern family. I wanted to honor what was there while making it work for my clients' urbane tastes. I already had a good idea of their likes and dislikes, but this was the country and called for a reframing of their tastes to suit

EQUESTRIAN HIDEAWAY

the environment. My job involved balancing the past and the present—figuring out what modern pieces would work in the context of a nineteenth-century farmhouse, as well as what traditional pieces needed to be layered in to make it look cohesive.

As with most houses of the era, it had been added to over time here and there, resulting in a mix of woodwork and finishes. To make things more consistent and seamless, I had some moldings replaced to streamline the look and ebonized the existing wide-plank oak floor. By honoring yet updating these elements, the original character was maintained, and the effect was both polished and charming. This design dialogue is introduced in the entry hall, where I highlighted the trim in a historically correct blue and covered the walls in a horizontally striped wallpaper for a bit of fun. For the art, we wanted an updated version of the customary horse paintings, so we opted for a large-scale photo of a detail of a horse by Steven Klein, a contemporary photographer who loves and raises horses himself.

The living room appears to be the most traditional room in the house, though none of the furniture in it is actually traditional. The subdued, neutral palette creates this impression, as do the roughhewn beams and rustic fire surround, but a

DEDAR MILANO

close look reveals a converging of periods. Again, the moldings are painted blue, and the rug gives the room a bright ground. The sofas and other furnishings have modernized profiles, more commonly found in Park Avenue apartments than in century-old farmhouses.

As it's a home for spending time with the family, we created a large, open kitchen/dining room, perfect for family breakfast, entertaining friends, and meeting with the groomsmen from the stables. The cabinetry has clean lines and, with lots of gleaming silver appliances, it doesn't feel period at all. Although not ornate, the materials are of the finest quality—cabinets of walnut and oak, and countertops of black and white granite. Running along a row of pretty windows, the long, narrow dining table has a glossy finish complemented by a buttery, tobacco-colored leather banquette seat cushion and orange leather pillows. To create just the right tension between the new and old, I hung a vintage print of a riding scene on the wall at the head of the table. Nearby, there's a small, circular table surrounded by plaid wing chairs and a clubby sofa for more intimate groups and cozy chats.

The media room, which was once the formal dining room, is swathed in a dark Ultrasuede fabric, which beautifully disguises the speakers. A metallic paper on the ceiling optically raises the room's height and bounces light around the otherwise dark space. The contemporary nature of a blocky orange sectional with oversized ottomans is balanced by ikat pillows. The library, furnished with generous leather chairs surrounding a card table and lined with built-in modern shelving backed in a rich red, has a more formal tone. The very modern pendant light is the perfect foil to the woodwork.

One of the most exciting spaces, to me, is the lounge. I love that the clients wanted a room for entertaining in a glamorous way even in the country. With that directive, I worked with Fromental to create a custom wallpaper on a very dark ground with overscale gilded leaves. To

PAGE 48 AND LEFT: Mood boards capture equestrian motifs counterbalanced by more urbane materials.

complement the gold, I found a jazzy Pierre Cardin sideboard in white with gold details that became the bar. The striped rug picks up on the rhythm of the leaves in the wallpaper, while a long banquette-style sofa extends the length of the room, with handy bolster pillows that can be moved around to break the space up into different conversation groups. In true cocktail-lounge fashion, a series of small, circular tables, perfect for resting martinis on, runs down the center of the narrow space.

Upstairs, the primary bedroom walks the line as well. A four-poster bed feels old-fashioned in spirit though its lines are incredibly clean. To bring the green of the tree leaves in from the outside, I chose a paper with an aloe-green ground that recalls a William Morris Arts and Crafts print but is a modern update. The cabinet is mid-century, whereas the chair, one that was historically used for removing riding boots, reprises the equestrian theme. The son's bedroom also mixes old and new by playing the exposed stone of the chimneypiece off the leather-clad bed. Here, I've added overscale reading lamps, which I find essential to have at arm's length from any bed.

I love to see how these friends and clients live in this home. They truly enjoy every room and have made a charming old house work with their cool, modern style.

RIGHT: The entrance drive sweeps through verdant horse pastures in Westchester County, New York.

PAGE 52: In the entry, the original floors were ebonized to contrast the trim painted in a historically accurate blue.

PAGE 53: An oversized horse photograph by Steven Klein establishes the retreat's equestrian nature as well as a dose of drop-dead chic.

PAGES 54–55: In the living room, there's a level of comfort and casualness along with a Liaigre bench and a François-Xavier Lalanne duck.

RIGHT: In the lounge, a long banquette punctuated with bolster pillows, a series of cocktail tables, and occasional chairs allow for myriad conversation clusters.

PAGE 58: A hand-painted wallcovering by Fromental brings nature into the entertaining space, and a Pierre Cardin sideboard provides the perfect place for mixing cocktails.

PAGE 59: On the mantel, Kidrobot collectible figures depict the Gorillaz virtual band.

PAGE 60: In the library, artfully arranged books and objects set against a red background create the feeling of an art installation.

PAGE 61: In the kitchen, an industrial table and chairs pop against ebonized floors and crisp white walls.

PAGE 62: Not your traditional farm kitchen: in the dining area, tartan wools mix with supple orange and tobacco-colored leather for distinct seating options.

RIGHT: Once the formal dining room, the media room has walls covered in Ultrasuede and a metallic-papered ceiling.

PAGE 66: In the son's bedroom, original stonework accentuates the custom leather bed.

PAGE 67: A daybed in the home office provides a cozy reading nook.

LEFT: In the primary bedroom, the wallpaper recalls a William Morris print and brings in the greenery from outside, while a four-poster bed feels eternally classic.

WHEN A CLIENT CALLED UPON ME TO RENOVATE AND DECORATE A Bermuda-style house in South Florida, I was instantly taken by its charming approach to indoor-outdoor living. Although we took everything down to the studs, architect Mark Marsh of Bridges Marsh & Associates carefully rebuilt the home in line with the client's vision for adding a second story without losing any of its original simplicity. The rest of the team was equally skilled, with landscape firm Nievera Williams designing spectacular views seen from each window and Nathan Orsman adding flawless lighting.

A double-height foyer establishes the house's modernist bent. The straightforward lines and rhythmic spacing of a floating staircase recall the work of Donald Judd. From there, the floor plan's uncomplicated scheme unfolds, with rooms flowing into one another and indoors seamlessly merging with outdoors. The living and dining areas occupy one large room, which adds to the laid-back feeling of the design. A sculptural table with a geometric base from Egg Collective offers versatility; it can serve as a foyer table for books and favorite objects, a buffet table for an informal dinner, or a dining table that seats twelve. The other half of the space features an

MODERN TRANQUILLITY

arrangement of sofas and chairs, all with low backs, allowing for unobstructed ocean views. Every piece was selected to be useful, sculptural, and lighthearted.

The living area effortlessly transitions into the kitchen, which is polished enough to welcome guests. My client prefers a casual approach to entertaining at the beach, and this design is ideally suited for that. Blackened-steel cabinets with brass insets, swaths of beautifully grained walnut, and marble countertops and center island are complemented by Finn Juhl chairs upholstered in a buttery leather. All in all, it's a highly tactile and deeply sophisticated place to cook and dine in. The media room, also just off the living area, gives the family a place to congregate and watch television. The custom white oak millwork presents an entire wall for displaying books and collectible items from travels, including Japanese wicker antiques and African head rests.

The bedrooms bring elements of color into the home. I designed a pair of his-and-her guest bedrooms with the same headboards, curtain and wall fabrics, benches, and rugs—one in blue and the other in pink. Although the accessories and bedside tables differ, the concept is really an unexpected take on my hotel projects.

1034

The rooms have a cozy feeling without being fussy or overly busy. The primary bedroom occupies the same footprint as the living room below, so it's quite expansive. I carved the space into two smaller areas by using the headboard to divide the room and placing the bed in the middle of the side looking out to the ocean. On the opposite side is an inviting seating area that's perfect for reading the paper in the morning or watching the television hidden in the headboard at the end of the day. But perhaps the most remarkable feature is the room's bright marigold hue. At first the client was skittish, thinking it would be way too much color, but I assured her that it wouldn't seem overwhelming when broken up by the neutral color of the tray ceiling and ivory rug, and would feel like sunshine—which it absolutely does.

Of course, given the location of the house, some of the most interesting rooms are outside. The winter porch, in a palette of neutral materials, including limestone, cast concrete, and wood, is a frequent gathering spot next to the infinity pool. There's also a Zen garden—a private sanctuary featuring pebbles, geometric pavers, palm trees, and a sculptural marble tub. And that's exactly what this type of getaway home should be—the ultimate escape, where everything harmonizes and beautifully comes together.

PAGE 71 AND LEFT: Art, color, and textures contribute to the spirited mood boards for a South Florida home.

PAGE 74: In the dining area of the living/dining room, a sculptural table from Egg Collective serves multiple functions.

PAGE 75: In the living area, Swedish porcelain vases sit atop a bronze table by Laverne.

PAGES 76–77: Furnishings in muted tones, including Vladimir Kagan chairs, a bronze table by Laverne, and French ceramic lamps from the 1950s, bring a tranquil mood to the living area.

PAGES 78–79: An array of low-backed seating gives way to the spectacular view across the lawn to the ocean.

COUNTRY & SEASIDE • 75

PAGES 80-81: In the media room, a chaise-style sofa provides cozy seating for evenings in front of the television, which is encased in custom millwork made of white oak.

LEFT: A walnut and marble kitchen island is paired with Finn Juhl chairs. Blackened-steel, glass-fronted cabinets with bronze insets display simple yet elegant glassware and white dinnerware.

PAGES 84-85: In the "his" guest bedroom, a Gio Ponti cabinet emphasizes the blue theme, and a bench in the style of Tommi Parzinger is upholstered in a striped fabric that echoes the cabinet's blue and white paneling.

PAGES 86-87: The complementary "her" guest bedroom, in muted shades of pink, is accessorized with feminine chintz pillows.

PAGES 88-89: In the primary bedroom, a marigold palette creates the effect of sunshine. A concealed television rises out of the walnut headboard, which divides the spacious room.

PAGES 90-91: Matouk linens lend pattern and vivacity to the bedroom.

PAGE 92: Off the primary bedroom, a coffee bar, complete with a Saint Laurent marble countertop and a hidden refrigerator, allows the client to linger before heading downstairs in the morning.

PAGE 93: The adjacent dressing room is lined with walnut cabinetry inspired by Japanese shoji screens.

PAGE 94: With its double sink and rolled white towels, the white-lacquered primary bath has a spa-like vibe.

PAGE 95: A wall of book-matched marble creates a striking backdrop for a state-of-the-art shower.

PAGES 96–97: The winter porch, which leads out to the infinity pool, continues the house's color palette of variously textured neutral materials and rich use of wood.

LEFT: Near the gate that leads out to the beach, a solid marble tub is the focal point of a Zen garden.

CITY

MANY DESIGNERS MUST TRY TO CONVINCE CLIENTS TO GO ALONG WITH daring decisions, but for the revamp of a duplex in Soho, I was fortunate enough to work with a couple who are fun, fearless, and wild. I find that good things come when there's no holding back, and that was certainly the case with this project. In fact, a big part of my role involved figuring out a way to balance all their adventurous choices.

The pair wanted to create an oasis in the middle of the city, so I added Zen architectural details to the space, including a towering stair wall of geometrically carved wood and luxurious but minimalist furniture, such as the Cassina table in the kitchen and the Fendi sofas and chairs in the living room. They're also big entertainers and wanted options for places to host friends. In the main loft area, we inserted a bar. Not only does it make for a friendly welcome, but it partitions the kitchen from the rest of the living area.

We also created a personal nightclub in the duplex long before the pandemic made staying at home a trend. The spacious room is divided into his-and-her décor themes, creating separate areas for the couple to enjoy their individual pursuits. On his side, which is enveloped in cherrywood paneling, a generous Harvey Probber

ART LOVERS' LOFT

couch is paired with a Willy Rizzo table and accented with a Murakami painting. Her space is much more feminine with a curvy, tufted sofa, Molteni suede chairs, and an area for card games with a bar cart.

But the nightclub isn't the only place to entertain. Even more expansive is the outdoor area on the second floor. Past the Kaws figure on the stair landing lies a 3,000-square-foot terrace complete with seating covered in a red-and-black-striped Perennials fabric, a pergola draped with curtains, and festive chandeliers. Rectangular pavers edged with grass provide another striking graphic touch. The indoor spaces on this level follow suit. The dining area gets its energy from a patterned Rug Company carpet and an appropriation painting by Richard Pettibone. The television room has the same punchy rug and a seating fabric that reverses the stripe found outdoors. Not to mention the gym and accompanying alfresco hot tub.

The couple's passion for art is on display throughout the home, and we had fun tying the works back to the design. In the living room, a Damien Hirst butterfly work complements an Alexander McQueen butterfly floor covering. In the dining room, a vibrant Mel Bochner text piece served as the catalyst for the palette, which

includes purple Royère chairs, multicolored Damien Hirst spin plates, and hand-painted floor. Rare wood carvings by Keith Haring echo the wood of the stair wall. And I just love how a Mr. Brainwash screen print of Kate Moss gets even more turbocharged when hung atop a Brunschwig & Fils wallpaper that mimics the shelves of a library and camouflages a home office.

At every turn throughout this home, there is passion. It may come in the form of eye-catching art, strong colors, even boldly patterned rugs. The clients are drawn to furniture, fabrics, and art that say a lot, and they're not afraid to live that way. But my crucial task was to bring balance to the equation—allowing certain pieces to whisper so others can shout.

PAGE 103 AND LEFT: Mood boards for a downtown penthouse illustrate strong colors and dynamic patterns.

PAGE 106: A sculpture by KAWS on the landing contrasts with the textured, hand-carved stair wall.

PAGE 107: A butterfly-patterned Alexander McQueen rug for the Rug Company lays the groundwork in the living room.

PAGES 108-9: Artworks by Richard Prince and Damien Hirst bring color to the space.

RIGHT: Red leather seating brightens the kitchen.

PAGES 112–13: Hung between the windows, rare carvings by Keith Haring are just a few of the standout pieces in the owners' collection. A freestanding bar separates the kitchen from the rest of the living area.

PAGES 114–15: The dining room features a hammered-metallic wallpaper, a painting by Mel Bochner, Jean Royère chairs, and a hand-painted floor.

PAGES 116–17: On "her" side of the cherrywood-paneled lounge, a rug inspired by one created for a hallway in the Shelborne Hotel (see pages 170–91) creates a lively ground for generous suede seating and an Yves Klein coffee table.

PAGE 118: A painting by Carroll Dunham presides over a table for card games or intimate dinners.

PAGE 119: On "his" side, a Harvey Probber sofa and a Willy Rizzo table are paired with an artwork by Takashi Murakami.

PAGE 120: In the daughter's bedroom, textured paneling gives the space an Op Art vibe, as does the hanging plexiglass chair she requested.

PAGE 121: A Mr. Brainwash screen print featuring Kate Moss is mounted on a Brunschwig & Fils wallpaper that suggests a library and camouflages a home office.

LEFT: Lacquered blue walls enliven the primary bedroom suite, which does not receive much light.

PAGE 124: A dining space off the terrace, perfect for indoor picnics, is overlooked by a Richard Pettibone appropriation painting.

PAGE 125: The stylish gym features an outdoor hot tub.

RIGHT: The television room on the penthouse's second floor mirrors the spirit of the adjoining terrace.

PAGES 128-29: On the terrace, a curtained pergola frames an outdoor room. The sofas are upholstered in a red-and-black stripe that is the reverse of the fabric on the sofas in the adjacent television room. Beyond the pergola, rectangular pavers edged with grass add graphic interest.

Designing a home in an architectural marvel is any interior designer's dream. But when I was tasked with conceiving a family-friendly home in Tribeca's Herzog & de Meuron tower, affectionately known as the "Jenga" building, I quickly realized I was in for a challenge. The expansive apartment was all concrete and glass, filled with impressive engineering and sharp edges. It didn't exactly seem inviting for my clients, a young family, but I saw the opportunity for adaptation and applauded them for embracing the potential of such a cool space for raising their two children.

The first task was to map out the apartment. At almost 10,000 square feet, the wide-open floor plan needed to be carved up into places for adults and children to spend time both together and apart. The expansive living area had no visual separation, so I dissected it into smaller spaces. A rug defines the seating area, and a bar divides it from the dining area. Set on casters, the bar also pivots to reshape the layout as needed when entertaining. To give the parents privacy, I cordoned off the primary bedroom suite in its own wing, which is reached through a whimsical purple velvet door accented with nailheads.

A CUT ABOVE

Next, I had to address how to bring the clients' love of color into such a stark atmosphere. They were game to add it any- and everywhere, which I personally love. The living area took on a spice palette with tones of curry, paprika, and saffron. I swathed both the media room and the primary suite in shades of lapis and turquoise, the perfect complement to the skies beyond. In the kitchen, row upon row of cabinets in a rich cerulean hue top the exuberant backsplash, while a powder room was lacquered in an enchanting shade of plum.

Another client directive was the liberal use of stone. Incorporating this material didn't come as easily to me as color. The homeowners love expressively veined, rich marble—and who doesn't in a glamorous bath? But they envisioned it throughout their home. To keep things in the realm of family and far away from hotel lobby, I fulfilled their request in unexpected ways. In the entry, a parquet de Versailles floor is inset with a narrow band of marble. The wallpaper in the media room evokes a glittering geode, as does the malachite-patterned rug. I even found an opportunity for malachite fittings in the powder room. However, we did fully embrace their marble obsession in the master bath with some of the most interesting and expressive

examples I've ever seen. We book-matched a blue-and-brown Cassiopea specimen on the walls and floors to create an absolutely unforgettable bath.

Overall, every design decision came back to how to tone down the severity of the architecture. Double-faced curtains, purely a decorative touch since all the windows are outfitted with custom shades, soften the concrete columns. Soaring sixteen-foot ceilings feel less lofty coated in a warm gold leaf. Furniture is pulled in from the glass walls—adding a sense of connection in the cavernous spaces while accentuating the view. The interior walls of the primary suite were swathed in paper-backed fabric. In the daughter's room, walls of hand-painted flowers lend a sweetness, and in the son's space, vintage maps bring character. Some key art pieces add that last layer of personality and reflect the tastes of the family. A custom mural by Korean American artist Rostarr enlivens the entry. A Johanna Grawunder light installation dazzles above the dining table; nearby, a Manolo Valdés sculpture presides over the living area. But I've come to accept that even with all the rich colors, eye-catching design pieces, and works of art, as helicopters fly by at eye level, it's hard for the view not to steal the show.

PAGE 131 AND LEFT: Rich colors and extraordinary materials shaped the mood boards for this Tribeca apartment.

PAGE 134: In the entrance hall, a table designed by Ralph Rucci for Holly Hunt casts a striking silhouette against the Manhattan skyline. The floor is a modern take on parquet de Versailles.

PAGE 135: A sculpture by Manolo Valdés soars above the city.

PAGES 136-37: The living room and dining room occupy one large space, which a rolling bar cabinet can divide in multiple ways.

PAGE 138: A cocktail table by India Mahdavi plays off the colors in a work by Caio Fonseca hung on a wall covered in hand-painted Fromental grasscloth.

PAGE 139: An installation by Johanna Grawunder provides multiple options for lighting the dining table. The chairs have a cool, comfortable feeling with leather on the seats and a Tony Duquette fabric on the backs.

LEFT: The media room features a geode wallpaper and a malachite-patterned rug. The stepped-out wall conceals a ninety-inch television that lowers. The benches by Holly Hunt are covered in a faux ostrich, and the Ostrich floor lamp is by Hubert Le Gall.

PAGE 142: The open kitchen boasts a monumental hood by Anish Kapoor.

PAGE 143: In the breakfast area, a sinuous banquette and the Warren Platner chairs and table float in space to give way to the views.

PAGES 144–45: With its predominantly blue palette, the primary bedroom appears as one with the sky. Cerused-wood walls, dark walnut floors, and velvet upholstery add to the tranquil mood.

OPPOSITE: Book-matched marble on the walls and floor of the primary bath competes for attention with the stunning views, which can be admired from the spa-like tub.

RIGHT: The powder room is a jewel box with plum-colored lacquer walls, a Roll & Hill light fixture, and malachite and gold-plated fittings.

PAGE 148: A world map adds character to the young son's bedroom.

PAGE 149: A flower mural wraps the walls of the daughter's bedroom. Furniture that can be easily transformed and swapped out as she gets older was selected.

RECENTLY, I FOUND MYSELF SPENDING MORE AND MORE TIME IN PALM Beach. With multiple projects in the area, hotel hopping had lost its luster. Feeling the need to set up a more permanent base in Florida, I decided to rent an apartment on South Ocean Boulevard. The architecture of the building struck me as extraordinary. The footprint was set close enough to the water that the views from the sixth floor created the impression that you were floating on a yacht.

What was not as extraordinary were the interior furnishings supplied by a stager. It was instantly clear that most of it had to go, I needed to strike a balance between what was functional for a place that was not mine and surroundings that felt like me—even if it was just for the short term. The summer before, friends in the Hamptons who were renting a house for a few months explained that they had installed their own art collection in their rental. At the time I thought that was perhaps excessive, going far beyond bringing along your own sheets and pillows. But it now made perfect sense.

I made an inventory of what I could live with in the apartment and what simply could not and would not work. Culling pieces from the staged furnishings and add-

RENTAL REDO

ing artwork, select furniture items, and accessories that reflected my personal tastes, I developed a scheme that lived up to the building's groovy bones yet embodied an incredibly minimal sensibility, especially for me. After all, a lot of white goes a long way. So, the stager came to pick up my rejects, and I packed a truck in New York and headed down the coast.

Knowing that the foyer sets the tone for what follows, I had to clear the slate—bringing in a console I found at Ponce Berga on Dixie Highway in West Palm Beach, a pair of Eric Schmitt chairs, a David Hockney iPad drawing, and candlesticks from my Theodore Alexander collection. In the living room, the sofa and bench were already in place, but I pulled in the armchairs, which had been scattered throughout the apartment, then added an uplight from a vintage shop on Dixie Highway and a Charles Price wishbone on the cocktail table. The existing dining table got a makeover when I paired it with Finn Juhl chairs and cheered up the room with a colorful, reflective work by Jose Alvarez, an artist I had discovered while in town.

Given my personal passion for setting the table, stocking the pantry with my china and linens was a must. Linens I had picked up in Provence, colorful glassware

IT'S A
THING
CONDENSED

TOMATO
SPRAY

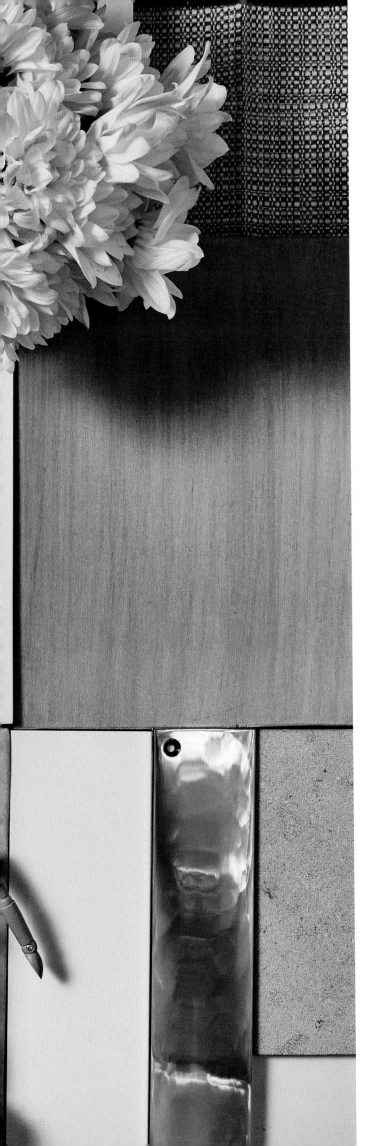

from my Hamptons house, Tory Burch spongeware, and placemats from Crate & Barrel brought life and warmth to every meal. What was even better was that it gave me the opportunity to use pieces that had been out of rotation in my day-to-day life.

That spirit of mixing permeated the bedrooms as well. In the primary suite, new furniture from Serena & Lily and Room & Board, a rug dragged from another space, and a sofa repositioned in the corner all felt more me, especially after I added favorite Matouk linens to the bed. In a guest bedroom, basically a blank canvas, a Rachel Lee Hovnanian neon work and a vintage chair from a shop on Dixie Highway packed some personality and punch.

The finished look was stripped-down minimalism, but everything that stood out was mine. Living with no color for a maximalist like me was certainly a departure, but I discovered a tranquillity from being in an uncluttered space that had the bare essentials I needed to feel comfortable. It was my version of living in a monastery, devoid of everything except a few stylish things. And in the end, I came away with my own revelation—with some creativity and effort you can feel right at home anywhere you go.

PAGE 151 AND LEFT: Mood boards of stark white mixed with pops of art and color capture the essence of this Florida project.

PAGE 154: A view of the beach from the apartment's floor-to-ceiling windows.

PAGE 155: In the foyer, a pair of Eric Schmitt chairs and a console from Ponce Berga on Dixie Highway are complemented by a David Hockney work.

PAGES 156–57: Although the furniture is all white, the blue of the sky and water introduce color into the living room. Accessories such as the Charles Price wishbone and small vases add personality to the otherwise minimalist space.

PAGE 158: Colorful glassware and ceramics, along with a simple Kartell bar cart, make daily breakfasts on the terrace a joy.

PAGE 159: Personal touches like a tablecloth from a trip to Provence make a rental feel like home.

LEFT TOP AND BOTTOM: My passion for setting the table ranges from casual linens with Tory Burch china at breakfast (top) to more formal embroidered napkins with Mottahedeh porcelain for lunch or dinner (bottom).

OPPOSITE: Finn Juhl chairs warm up a stark dining table, and a Jose Alvarez canvas brightens up the space, as does a colorful table setting.

PAGES 162–63: Matouk bedding adds character to the primary bedroom's collection of clean-lined furniture.

PAGE 164: A vintage chair found on Dixie Highway and a neon artwork by Rachel Lee Hovnanian lend a sense of cool to a guest bedroom.

PAGE 165: Fresh towels, an Alvar Aalto stool, and a woven animal head by Javier Sanches keep the bath from being too clinical.

PAGE 166: The office décor includes a pair of Olivetti chairs and a lamp from Visual Comfort.

PAGE 167: A few stylish accessories is all the kitchen needs to feel welcoming.

LIFESTYLE

Growing up in the 1960s, I remember vacationing in Miami Beach with my family. Even as a young child, I was enchanted by the glamour and enthralled by the design of the stylish hotels. Among those glitzy Miami Modern destinations, the Eden Roc, the Fontainebleau, and the Shelborne always stood out in my mind. All created by architect Morris Lapidus, this trio, with their whiplash curves and aura of kitsch, left me in awe. The Eden Roc was the most exclusive, the hotel of choice of the Rat Pack when they were in town. Frank Sinatra, Dean Martin, and the gang could all be found in its cocktail lounge, and the rooms were known for their split-level suites and terrazzo floors. The performances took place at the Fontainebleau, a few doors down, which was the largest and defied architectural understatement with its faux-French air. Lapidus once said of these projects, "I wanted people to walk in and drop dead."

Although originally built in 1941 by another firm, the Shelborne was expanded in 1958 by Lapidus, who brought his brand of what an architecture critic of the day referred to as "tail-fin chic" to the hotel. His overhaul included the addition of eight stories, as well as the property's iconic, neon-lit porte cochere. So, when the oppor-

SOUTH BEACH SHOWSTOPPER

tunity to work on a redesign came my way, I jumped at the chance. After an intense round of presentations, I beat out a field of nearly thirty other firms with my promise to give the destination a feeling of modern luxury while preserving its ties to the past.

The first thing to note when beginning to work on a project of this kind is that the building was landmarked. The rooms had to remain the same size, and no walls could be moved. Over the last half century, the expectations of the scale of a hotel room have markedly changed, so it was up to me to figure out how to put every square inch to excellent use, almost as if I were designing a yacht.

Knowing these would never be the largest rooms in South Beach by any stretch of the imagination, I set out to make them the coolest ones. All 290 rooms, in a variety of configurations, called for healthy doses of inspiration, so I pulled from a number of sources. Of course, the original hotel and its Miami Modernism history was a major one, but I also wove in elements from my favorite hotel in the world, the Parco dei Principi in Sorrento, created by Italian architect and designer Gio Ponti in 1961. I used a large-scale version of his tile pattern for the carpets in the rooms and one of his classic furniture designs for the desks. As the headboards

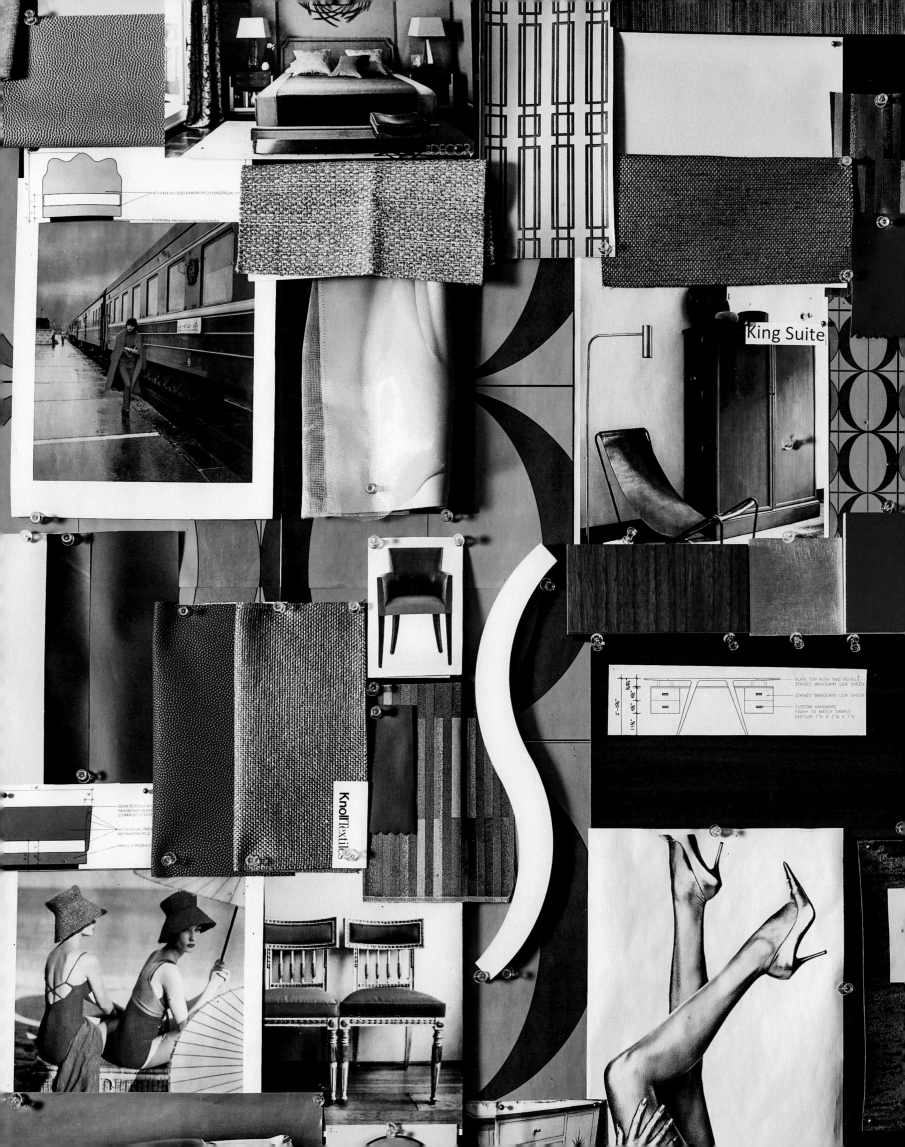

King Suite

Knoll Textiles

Meeting Rooms

had to be vinyl to withstand wear and tear, I gave them a sinuous shape to add character instead of relying on fancy fabric. For the larger suites, I designed minibars with hand-painted sunbursts, based on a piece of furniture by Dorothy Draper, who designed the hotel's original ballroom. I made them a little wilder by using bicycle reflectors for the drawer pulls, rather than the usual bronze or crystal. In a nod to mid-century style, I hung my own simplified versions of Tommi Parzinger mirrors. The bathrooms got their own retro touch with a modernized version of an Albert Hadley motif done as vinyl wallpaper.

The hallways proved to be another fantastic place to set the mood and recall the hotel's illustrious history. I worked the "S" of the Shelborne logo into the carpet pattern and winked at other elements of the fabulous entrance drive with design choices. I chose lighting that looked like headlights on antique cars and used automotive paint for the doors, which is also extremely resistant to scratches and dings from luggage. The ceiling was painted blue, another nod to Ponti, to suggest the sky. So, the hallways in some ways were transformed into outdoor streets.

The vestibule and hallway leading to the Draper ballroom was a big part of the project as well. I lined the vestibule with some of Draper's original shell sconces, which had been preserved. The walls had once been lacquered, but as that kind of lavish expense was not in the budget, I opted for a patent-leather wallcovering instead. To harken back to days gone by, I used blown-up photography of jazz instruments and musicians. The carpeting I designed for the hallway recalls the waves in the Macassar ebony used for the bookcase and sheathing the columns—but also does heavy lifting in hiding the spills and accidents that are bound to happen. And I couldn't resist having the original double doors leading into the space re-created.

Outside, the waterfall diving board still reigns over the pool, which I surrounded with cabanas that have a groovy, Jetsons feel. Filled with nostalgia for my childhood,

PAGE 171 AND LEFT: Bringing together old and new was central to the mood board presented to the team at the Shelborne Hotel.

I could never have imagined then that I would work on this Lapidus building, adding my own sense of style. But working on a hotel is so much more than just creating a pretty backdrop. Budget and performance are as critical to the final product as is working as a team. It's an exercise in collaborating with people, jointly coming up with design ideas, but in the end you're ultimately responsible for making it the hundred different things it needs to be. We revived as much of the past as we could, to give guests a sense that they're going back in time—all while feeling very now.

ABOVE: Towering palms in planters that are part of the original architecture add a touch of retro glamour to the pool.

RIGHT: The porte cochere at the Shelborne Hotel is an icon of Miami Modern design.

PAGE 176: I re-created the doors to the ballroom, originally designed by Dorothy Draper.

PAGE 177: A Macassar ebony bookcase near the ballroom, now a conference room, allows companies to display accessories themed to their presentation or brand.

LEFT: In the vestibule near the former ballroom, a patent-leather wallcovering recalls the original lacquered walls, original Dorothy Draper sconces have been repurposed, and large-scale photography of musical instruments evokes the Rat Pack era.

OPPOSITE: Guest-room corridors are designed to feel like busy city streets with glossy car-paint doors, headlight-style sconces, and sky-blue ceilings.

PAGES 180–81: If the architecture is landmarked, as the Shelborne's is, the floor plans of the diminutive bedrooms must take advantage of every square inch.

PAGE 182: The pattern of the carpet in the guest rooms was inspired by Gio Ponti tilework.

PAGE 183: Minibars recall furniture designed by Dorothy Draper, and mirrors pay tribute to Tommi Parzinger.

PAGES 184–85: Kitschy accessories harken back to the hotel's mod 1960s origins.

PAGE 186: Sheers should always be white and let in clear light but block the sun.

PAGE 187: Graphic patterns bring life to the rooms with starbursts on the furniture, circles on the floor, and rectangles on the wallpaper.

RIGHT: Similar design elements are employed across multiple types of rooms.

PAGE 190: Simple white bathrooms feel clean and fresh in hotels.

PAGE 191: The curves of the headboards add a mid-century Italian flair.

As a child growing up in Bogotá, I spent my winters in Cartagena, the enchanting city along Colombia's Caribbean coast. It's a magical place, and I love visiting the sixteenth-century house I restored in the center of the old city with my wife, children, and friends. Creating our home in this UNESCO heritage site, I learned to balance stringent preservation guidelines with my love for both antiquity and modernity—along with a healthy dose of local inspiration. That's why I was flattered but not totally surprised when the wildly talented fashion designer Silvia Tcherassi asked to visit my house to glean ideas for a new hotel she was working on. I had an even better idea—I proposed to design the fifty-room hotel myself and become a partner in the adventurous project named Hotel Tcherassi.

Having already worked with the local landmarks committee, which fiercely guards the centuries-old buildings within the old, walled city, I knew my limitations, but that did not stop me from letting my imagination run wild. I conjured a story of the Spanish royals coming to the New World for a visit. Legend has it that Queen Isabella was always promising to make the journey and kept sending all her gorgeous trunks back and forth. Although the trip ultimately never happened,

REWRITING HISTORY

her baggage is on display in a local museum—and that's how I decided to make the check-in desks replicas of those fabulous, oversized artifacts. The surrounding Spanish *zaguán,* or arched foyer, retains its original, sixteenth-century wood beams and walls, which I left with bits of peeling stucco unpatched. Local mirrors in a gold tone recall the stories of El Dorado, which purported that the surface of a lake was entirely covered with gold dust. And I couldn't help but call on Soicher Marin to reproduce portraits of the Spanish royals to make the effect complete.

Light pours into the open-air space, which leads out to a hanging garden created by Silvia's mother, Vera, who is a noted horticulturist. With the humidity and sunshine, the array of local species thrived, and the courtyard is now so dense that guests can't see from balcony to balcony. I'm especially fond of the little boats accenting the water feature, which I think of as a nod to the canoes plying the rivers in search of the Lost City of Gold.

For the design of the guest rooms, I decided to go against type. Since everything in Cartagena is super colorful, I thought, why not stick with white, beige, and ivory. There's something so calming about checking into an uncluttered hotel room,

where you can immediately see that everything is clean. To achieve this look without sacrificing a luxurious feel, I had minimal-yet-interesting furniture made in the spirit of Charlotte Perriand by Colombian craftsmen. Chairs and stools upholstered in hammock fabric, as well as photos of the old city, provide some splashes of color. A few curated items go a long way to elevate the look. Accessories, including baskets I had woven in color palettes pulled from Mark Rothko paintings, along with hats and sarongs, add more brightness and local flair as well. If you want to be minimalist, you can infuse your space with a few special pieces to create texture and a sense of luxury. It also helps keep within a budget, which is essential for projects of this type.

When I look at this hotel and what it represents, I'm filled with pride. I think of it as my gift to Cartagena—representing a modernist vision of the city while paying homage to its centuries-old legacy. From the original lock on the front door to the throw on the foot of the bed, every element tells a part of the hotel and the magical place it inhabits—a delicate balance of past, present, and future.

PAGE 193 AND LEFT: Inspiration for the Tcherassi Hotel comes from Colombia's rich history and tradition of artisanal crafts.

PAGE 196: A collection of mirrors by local artisans bounces light around the entry to the hotel.

PAGE 197: Working within local preservation guidelines, I retained the original walls and beams in the foyer. The check-in desks are replicas of trunks that Queen Isabella of Spain sent in advance of a planned journey to the New World—a trip that never happened.

LEFT: A mix of old and new comes together in a seating area with reproductions of portraits of the Spanish royals and contemporary furnishings.

PAGES 200-201: The fifty guest rooms embrace a new vision of design in Cartagena—using the work of local artisans in fresh and modern ways, including the woven fabric on the cubes.

RIGHT: A palette of white dotted with sparse color accents gives the guest rooms a crisp, clean look. Closets are vented to keep clothing fresh in the humidity.

PAGE 204: Hammock fabric on the chairs provides some of the only color in the room, although the hanging garden outside creates a verdant view.

PAGE 205: The atrium's hanging garden features boat-shaped planters that recall the canoes that explorers used to ply the rivers in their vain search for the lost city of El Dorado.

PAGES 206-7: Cartagena is a city of vibrant colors and patterns, so a white room offers a place to rest and reset.

LEFT: With a television that rises out of a console in the center of the room, the floor plan is freed up for a desk and more living space.

PAGE 210: The bathroom is accessorized with baskets made by local craftspeople.

PAGE 211: Doors lacquered with car paint add splashes of color in the hallways.

WHEN IT COMES TO RESTAURANT DESIGN, CLIENTS CAN BE VERY SPECIFIC about their needs. They might want it to be cozy and casual or romantic and intimate, maybe even large and boisterous. The designer must heed the particular vibe that the client wants the space to evoke. The floor plan plays a big part in realizing the restaurateur's vision, as do the decoration and accessories.

But when the owner of the Renaissance Hotel in Midtown Manhattan approached me about working with him on a new rooftop restaurant, I was given no such direction. Instead, I was asked to make the place basically everything from cozy and romantic to large and boisterous—and more. Located near Madison Square Garden, an area teeming with sports bars, there was a real opportunity to elevate the notion of what a sports bar could be. In addition, art fairs such as the Latin American Pinta Art Show are mounted nearby, so the restaurant could also serve collectors and gallerists during those busy weeks. And as the venue isn't far from the Garment District, creating a place to host fashion shows made sense as well. My client, both an art collector and a sports enthusiast, with a wife who is very into fashion, saw the opportunity to make this restaurant the perfect place for all these worlds to come

VICE VERSA

together—for events big and small, as well as business lunches and date nights. The restaurant would be called Versa in homage to its amazing versatility.

Never one to shy away from a challenge, I tackled the project head on—thinking of it as an exercise in creativity. How could a space serve such a diverse clientele? The result is a mashup of ideas that strike a balance, making the look cohesive, considered, and chic. Basing the entry on the owner's interest in art, I designed a wallpaper of blank frames inspired by the contemporary artist Allan McCollum, who is famous for his *Plaster Surrogates* series—each a cluster of black-and-white plaster models of picture frames, and one of which is in the permanent collection of the Museum of Modern Art. My interpretation includes a pattern of frames rendered in gold, black, and white to set the tone for the space and lend it a certain cool factor. As you move through the space, the wallpaper morphs into a black-and-white version, on which I've hung brightly painted frames for an added dimension. Layering vibrant color on top of a black-and-white ground is a surefire way to make it pop.

In the bar area, the themes of art and repetition continue with cabinets filled with small, shiny dog sculptures after Jeff Koons. Not only are they fun but their

reflective nature bounces light from within the more serious millwork. Above the bar, a series of TV screens gives the restaurant that sports-bar feel, albeit an elevated one in which the atmosphere changes when the programming changes. The televisions can just as easily play runway shows or a series of art slides as the Super Bowl. Nearby, the open seating area has a more formal atmosphere than the bar. In a nod to fashion, I covered the chair backs in an intricate fabric with a variety of motifs running through it vertically, piped the seats in navy, and upholstered the fronts in a really soft white leather. Such sophisticated detailing signals that this isn't your typical sports bar or function hall.

The most dynamic space is undoubtedly the open-air terrace, which can be covered by an enormous retractable roof. When the roof is open, diners are seated right under the Empire State Building with the magnificent Midtown skyline surrounding them. Hedges in movable containers give the space a bit of an English garden atmosphere and can be shifted around to carve the space into different configurations. You can line them up for a fashion show or wall off an area for a private cocktail hour or business presentation—the options are limitless. There are also semi-private cabanas with tables that seat up to fourteen people; maximally flexible, they can be scaled up or down, depending on the function, from business meetings during the day to lounge areas throughout the evening.

This space had to function in so many ways, and by adding elements of movability to my floor and furniture plans and using design themes and motifs with crossover appeal, Versa has truly become a restaurant for everyone and anyone, no matter what their needs. When I look back on it, I think I really designed about ten incredible restaurants in one.

PAGES 213 AND LEFT: Fashion, sports, and art converge in the mood boards for the restaurant Versa.

PAGE 216: In the entry, a wallpaper of blank frames verges on an art installation in and of itself.

PAGE 217: In the dining room, another colorway of the wallpaper is layered with frames painted in bright colors.

PAGES 218-19: Cabinet after cabinet of the Jeff Koons–inspired dogs add a sense of whimsy while touching on the restaurant's art influence.

OPPOSITE: A mix of patterned textiles on counter stools is a reflection of the restaurant's location near the Garment District.

RIGHT TOP AND BOTTOM: Restaurant bathrooms are perfect opportunities to surprise guests with bold design elements.

PAGES 222-23: The dining room is one of the more formal spaces in the multi-room restaurant.

VERSA
WINE BAR

VERSATILE SELECTIONS

BY THE GLASS

HALF BOTTLES

CORAVIN

BY THE BOTTLE

ASK YOUR BARTENDER
FOR WEEKLY POUR
#VERSANYC

RIGHT: On the open-air terrace, movable walls of hedges divide the space into semi-private seating arrangements that work as well for business meetings as they do for private parties.

PAGES 226-27: The furniture and greenery on the rooftop terrace can be rearranged to create runways for fashion shows and private areas for special events.

PAGE 228-29: Light wood mixed with dark accents and patterned tile creates a refined sports-bar setting.

DESIGN CONCEPTS

WHEN IT COMES TO SHOW HOUSES, THERE'S NO QUESTION THAT THE annual Kips Bay Decorator Show House in New York is the mother of them all. Being invited to participate is such an honor, but also a tremendous responsibility. The first time I was asked, I was assigned what was basically a closet and small passageway to decorate. I transformed the meager space into a veritable jewel box and have since gone on to design six others. Most recently, in 2017, I was given the living room, usually the largest, most challenging space in the house and seen as the prize assignment.

Successfully executing an installation of this scale requires a firm commitment to a solid inspiration. In this case, I turned to one of the greatest of all time, the Italian interior designer, architect, and set designer Renzo Mongiardino, who reigned as the go-to of the world's most fashionable clients in the 1970s and 1980s. I pored over images of the divine Hôtel Lambert, which he designed for Marie-Hélène de Rothschild in Paris, among other transportive projects. In no way did I seek to copy his groundbreaking style; instead, I set about imagining what the legendary designer would create now—how he would wield his power today to create an aes-

MODERNIZING MONGIARDINO

thetic landscape. My major takeaway was that everything had to be artisanal and handcrafted—from the boldest gesture to the smallest accent.

For starters, the room needed a sense of history, something Mongiardino had a knack for conjuring and imposing on even the most architecturally dull hallway. I turned to Iksel, the brilliant wallcovering firm known for its astonishing prints. We created a scenic, digitally printed paper that combined layers of patterns, moldings, and marble detail. To me, it seemed the perfect modern-day answer to upholstered or hand-painted walls. We referenced the Aleppo Room, a sixteenth-century wood-paneled space now on display at the Pergamon Museum in Berlin. To our version of that room's iconic walls, we added borders on top and bottom, as well as a pattern of Persian miniatures in the panels surrounding the Hervé Van der Straeten sconces.

With the envelope in place, I went about filling the room with furnishings, art, and accessories just as rich and layered as the walls. Following in Mongiardino's footsteps, I decided that everything I chose had to be handcrafted, but the pieces had to be designed by artisans working today to keep the space from resembling a period remake. Brooklyn-based plaster artist Stephen Antonson created the chandelier,

accented with white-on-white Fortuny lightshades. A 120-year-old Persian rug, laid atop sisal, made for an elegant floorcovering. I had the cocktail tables hand-made in Brooklyn and gave them an Orientalist shape as a nod to the designer as well. Other pieces of note include a Mattia Bonetti bronze chair, Rose Tarlow tables, Simon Pearce hand-blown hurricane vases, and cachepots by Olivier Gagnère from Édition Limitée in Paris. Channeling Yves Saint Laurent's aesthetic, I included a mirror from Maison Gerard by Bill Willis, the great Tennessee-born designer who birthed what we think of as the globally chic Moroccan style, including the fashion designer's Marrakech home, Villa Oasis, as well as a little cerused-oak table I snapped up at the Saint Laurent auction.

For the artwork, Mongiardino loved including studies of animals by John James Audubon, so I used a Walton Ford, whom I consider the Audubon of our times. The large work by him proved to be the perfect focal point above the thirteen-foot-long couch covered in velvet from Kravet. Other pieces that add personality include a small Jean Cocteau of a soldier and a charcoal by Colombian painter Luis Caballero. I also turned to Soicher Marin to reproduce some Orientalist paintings. They're a great resource for reproducing old works and beautifully framing them. But truly, I consider all the details just as artful—the over-the-top Samuel & Sons tassels, the African stool turned table from Karl Springer, and the Gabriella Crespi vase filled with orchids.

All in all, the room was a beautiful testament to living in a layered, individual atmosphere made possible through works by artists and artisans I admire. There can't be enough said or written to express the importance of these creative talents to make unique environments. We must support them in their pursuits and celebrate their efforts, as we've seen far too many disappear over the years. Designers like me rely on them to turn our dreams into reality.

PAGE 233 AND LEFT: Inspiration for a Kips Bay Designer Show House living room includes designer Renzo Mongiardino, Fortuny fabrics, and a mother-of-pearl inlay box.

MODERN LUXURY   RICHARD MISHAAN
ARTFULLY MODERN   RICHARD MISHAAN

PAGES 236-37: Layer upon layer of furnishings, patterns, and art, including wallpaper by Iksel and a painting by Walton Ford, create the rich, well-traveled feeling of this living room.

OPPOSITE: Filled with elements of Old World luxuriousness, the room features wallpaper that re-creates the walls of a 600-year-old, hand-painted Syrian room and sofas upholstered in Bevilacqua velvet.

RIGHT: An ornately embroidered fabric transforms modernist slipper chairs from groovy into stately. The curtain fabric is dip-dyed, and the tassels from Samuel & Sons make the window treatments wonderfully over the top.

PAGES 240-41: An eclectic mix of Art Deco–inspired cabinets handmade in Brooklyn, a Mattia Bonetti chair, a mirror by Bill Willis from Maison Gerard, and Hervé Van der Straeten sconces creates a playful conversation about style and taste.

PAGE 242: When filling the open shelves of a cabinet to create visual interest, a bar is always a good place to start, as are old and new books, interesting ceramics, and collections of unexpected objects.

PAGE 243: A blue vase by Peter Schlesinger, a Gabriella Crespi vase filled with orchids, and small sculptures from the Metropolitan Museum of Art gift shop adorn a trio of tables; the one at the right was acquired from the Yves Saint Laurent auction.

When *Galerie* magazine invited me to participate in their first-ever show house, I jumped at the chance. Not only was the house in Sag Harbor, not far from my own home in the Hamptons, but the project promised to be unlike any other show house in its mission to bring together the worlds of art and design. Since that magical combination is very much at the heart of everything that I create, the opportunity seemed more than ideal.

When I was assigned the primary bedroom suite, I didn't initially realize the full extent of the space. It quickly became apparent, however, that I would be taking on not only the rather grand bedroom but also a vestibule, a walk-in closet, and an outdoor terrace. Excited by the prospect of carving out so many distinct moments within the larger space, I began scheming.

I like to think of show houses as design labs, where I can experiment with some of the ideas that have been bubbling up in my head. Usually, they are the very types of ideas you don't try with clients because there's a chance they may fail. Of course, many more people will see the results of a show house than those of a private home, but I find it exhilarating that it's riskier, so I take bigger chances.

FIT FOR A KING

At a recent design conference in Nantucket, I learned the history of toile de Jouy. Although toile has now become a generic term for a whole range of fabrics, it originated in the eighteenth century in Jouy-en-Josas, a town just outside Versailles, where Christophe-Phillippe Oberkampf printed pastoral scenes on cotton. The reigning monarch at the time, King Louis XV, was known for his love of constantly changing the spaces around him. For example, one day he would order the orangerie to be filled with orange trees, only to have them switched to lemon trees the next. He even devised a way to quickly redecorate his bedchamber. He came up with the idea of having fabric hung on hooks, so it could easily be swapped out: tapestries in the winter, and different toiles in the warmer months. Riffing on that concept, I decided to slipcover the entire room in the Hamptons, where the high humidity can yellow upholstered walls.

For the fabric, I worked with my dear friend Lisa Fine. We scaled up one of her designs to make it more modern, and I added trim from Schumacher. For the niche surrounding the bed and the underside of the canopy, I used a striped fabric and two other trims to differentiate the space. In keeping with the theme, the covering of the

headboard also worked as a slipcover, complete with ribbons that allowed the width and length to be adjusted. The bed linens continued the blue-and-white-patterned motif. Over the bed, I hung a painting by Jane Freilicher that I borrowed from Kasmin Gallery. It was only after I hung it that I realized the landscape perfectly mirrored the glorious view of the pond outside.

Three other large artworks animated the space. Right before the installation, I went to see the Hockney show at the Royal Academy of Arts in London. I couldn't get his bright, mesmerizing iPad drawings out of my mind, so I used three in this space—their modern whimsy popping against the more traditional toile backdrop.

The overall effect proved to be so impactful that I didn't have to stuff the space with furniture. Instead, I chose a few exceptionally cool pieces such as an Achille Salvagni commode from Maison Gerard, which I paired with chairs from my own living room. That eclectic mix is also reflected in how I accessorized the shelves—including pieces of a dismantled tulipière; a painting of a clam by my wife, Marcia; hurricane candles from my collection with Theodore Alexander; and quirky blue gourds.

The whole space represents how ideas change, grow, and change again before they take final shape. I'm not certain that the king of France had this in mind when he decided to create wall hangings for his room, but centuries later, visitors to the show house were certainly intrigued. I even left a little flap open so they could pull back the fabric and literally peek behind the curtain.

PAGE 245 AND LEFT: Layers of fresh pattern, including Lisa Fine fabric, Schumacher trim, and Fromental wallpaper, inspired the mood boards for a Sag Harbor bedroom.

PAGE 248: A mirror by Hubert Le Gall and a hand-painted Fromental wallcovering blur the lines between old and new.

PAGE 249: The shift in scale between the bold floral wallpaper lining the vestibule leading into the primary bedroom suite and the delicate Lisa Fine floral fabric on the bedroom walls is dramatic.

PAGES 250–51: A pair of David Hockney iPad drawings surmount a cabinet by Achille Salvagni from Maison Gerard. The orchids are planted in an ice bucket by Gaetano Pesce, and the chairs are from my New York living room and were originally done by Mark Hampton. The horse sculpture is by Barry Flanagan, whose work is shown at Kasmin Gallery.

RIGHT: A painting by Jane Freilicher hangs above the bed, which is dressed in Schumacher fabrics for Matouk. The striped fabric is also by Schumacher, and the swing-arm lamps are by Circa.

PAGES 254–55: Custom cabinetry by Florense frames an iPad drawing by David Hockney.

PAGE 256: A cabinet niche is filled with the parts of a deconstructed ceramic tulipière.

PAGE 257: A custom closet by Florense is outfitted with quilted-leather paneling and drawer fronts.

PAGES 258–59: Swivel chairs by Bernhardt surround a firepit on the terrace off the bedroom.

When I was asked to participate in a charity show house at the W Hotel and Residences in Lower Manhattan, I was excited for the opportunity to see what I could come up with for a small one-bedroom apartment. I started by imagining a young guy living downtown with a lot of style but without a big budget. In hindsight, the results seem a little crazy but totally fun. I love that aspect of show houses—the chance to experiment with ideas you might never try on clients.

The entry really sets the stage for the entire apartment. I'm a huge fan of Sol LeWitt wall drawings. With their immersive quality, they bring you into the artwork and can make even the most nondescript space unforgettable. My thinking was, what would someone do if they loved those LeWitts but couldn't afford one. So I cut up a black-and-white-striped Serena & Lily wallpaper and had the installer hang it in a pattern. To add even more Op Art punch, I had graphics blown up and framed as paintings. Layered on top of the already kicky walls, these works became even more interesting. Although very "do-it-yourself" in spirit, the overall effect was bold, powerful, and, yes, unforgettable—exactly what I was looking for.

STARTER STYLE

I happened to be working on the Shelborne Hotel in South Beach around the same time (see pages 170–91). With all the imagery and ideas about the Rat Pack and that era of glamour swirling in my head, I decided to pick up on the "Chairman of the Board" as kind of a theme. I had a classic Frank Sinatra photograph printed at a large scale on laminate—yet another adventure in very affordable art. I've always wanted to experiment with ombré, so for the backdrop I worked with a specialty painter to create the look on the wall. When he pulled out cans of spray paint to execute the dip-dye effect, I was a little taken aback, but the result was stunning. The living room's furniture aligns with that era: a Tommi Parzinger sofa I snapped up at a Rago auction online, mid-century-inspired chairs, a card table in a corner, and the indispensable bar cart. I love styling bar carts; they are such an opportunity to show off individual taste and personality in the choice of gorgeous drinkware, fun barware, unique cocktail napkins, and even hard-to-find liquor brands.

In the bedroom, I circled back to the black-and-white-stripe motif to create a little drama, even though it took on a bit of a Dr. Seuss vibe. Why not? Having the

stripes climb around that Parzinger bed was just too much fun not to do, especially when you throw in the patterned rug fashioned from FLOR carpet tiles. For the floating bedside tables, I turned to one of my favorite resources for cost-conscious design: CB2. For one of the closets, I decided a secret gym would be the ultimate amenity. So, voilà—you pull the curtain back to find a TRX suspension system and a punching bag.

The apartment turned out to be the kind of bachelor pad a much younger version of myself would have loved to live in. It challenges me to work within budgets and push the concept and composition to do the heavy lifting instead of relying on expensive art and materials.

PAGE 261 AND LEFT: Punchy Op Art–inspired ideas dominate mood boards for the W Show House.

PAGES 264-65: The living room conjures the Rat Pack with a Tommi Parzinger sofa, a standing lamp from Circa, and a blown-up image of Frank Sinatra on a custom-painted wall. A work by Richard Serra hangs between the windows.

PAGES 266-67: By hanging a black-and-white-striped Serena & Lily wallpaper in an imaginative way, the entire entry becomes an Op Art installation inspired by Sol LeWitt.

PAGE 268: All the makings of a home gym are tucked into a closet.

PAGE 269: A Tommi Parzinger bed is surrounded by Serena & Lily wallpaper. Above the bed are flag paintings from Soicher Marin.

ACKNOWLEDGMENTS

I dedicate this book to my family, all of whom have given me the strength and courage to be who I am. To Marcia, Nicholas, and Alexandra for being the brutal critics you are and guiding me toward excellence.

Special mention goes to the late photographer George Ross. May he long be remembered for his exceptional vision and talent. He raised the bar in his field and made me expect nothing less. We miss you and are honored that you are a part of this book.

A heartfelt thank you to the homeowners of the projects featured in the book, both for the pleasure of working with you and for your permission to include your homes in the book.

I am deeply grateful to many people not only for their help in the creation of this book but also for their inspiration through the years.

FRIENDS WHO INSPIRE ME

Beth de Woody
Tiffany Dubin
Lisa Fine
Paul Kasmin
Eva Lorenzotti
Patty McEnroe
Dr. Brian Saltzman
Marlaine Selip
Claude Wasserstein

MAGAZINE EDITORS

Amy Astley
Michael Boodro
Pamela Fiori
Pamela Jaccarino
Whitney Robinson
Margaret Russell
Richard David Story
Jacqueline Terrebonne
Stellene Volandes

STYLISTS

Carolyn Englefield
Parker Larson
Robert Rufino
Anita Sarsidi

ARTISTS AND GALLERIES

Annely Juda Fine Art Gallery
Bernd Goeckler
Carpenters Workshop Gallery
David Gill
Diane de Polignac Art Gallery
Kasmin Gallery
KAWS
Magen H Gallery
Maison Gerard
Manolo Valdés

PHOTOGRAPHERS

Douglas Friedman
Genevieve Garruppo
Max Kim-Bee
Francesco Lagnese
Thomas Loof
George Ross

SPECIAL THANKS

Galerie Magazine Show House
Kips Bay Decorator Show House

MY BOOK TEAM

Thank you to Jill Cohen, a very special lady and friend who has guided and supported my vision for all three of my books. And to everyone at Vendome Press, especially Mark Magowan, Jim Spivey, Jacqueline Decter, and Susi Oberhelman. Finally, to my co-author and friend Jacqueline Terrebonne.

Richard Mishaan Design: Architecture and Interiors
First published in 2022 by The Vendome Press
Vendome is a registered trademark of The Vendome Press LLC

VENDOME PRESS US
P.O. Box 566
Palm Beach, FL 33480

VENDOME PRESS UK
Worlds End Studio
132-134 Lots Road
London, SW10 0RJ

www.vendomepress.com

Distributed in North America by Abrams Books
Distributed in the United Kingdom, and the rest of the world, by Thames & Hudson

ISBN 978-0-86565-412-9

Publishers: Beatrice Vincenzini, Mark Magowan, and Francesco Venturi
Editor: Jacqueline Decter
Production Director: Jim Spivey
Designer: Susi Oberhelman

Developed in conjunction with Jill Cohen Associates, LLC

Library of Congress Cataloging-in-Publication Data available upon request

Printed and bound in China by 1010 Printing International Ltd.

First printing

PHOTO CREDITS

George Ross: pp. 2–5, 50–53, 56–66, 174–91, 197–203, 205–7, 210–11, 216–29, 236–43, 264–69
Genevieve Garruppo: pp. 6–7, 19–21, 47–49, 71–99, 103–5, 131–33, 151–53, 171–73, 193–95, 213–15, 233–35, 245–59, 261–63
Thomas Loof: pp. 8, 134–49, 154–67
Max Kim-Bee: pp. 10–11, 106–29
Hernan Diaz: pp. 13, 15
Richard Mishaan: pp. 16, 100, 168, 230, 271
Francesco Lagnese: pp. 22–45, 196, 204–5
Will Waldron: pp. 54–55, 67–69
Douglas Friedman: pp. 196–203, 206–7, 208–11

PAGES 2–3: A living room inspired by Renzo Mongiardino.

PAGES 4–5: The sitting area of a downtown Manhattan apartment features a work by Richard Serra.

PAGES 6–7: A terrace in Sag Harbor offers an outdoor sanctuary off the primary bedroom suite.

PAGE 8: A Tribeca apartment with sweeping views gets its warmth from a rich color palette.

PAGES 10–11: A dining room in a downtown Manhattan penthouse combines bold art, color, and pattern.

PAGE 16: A sundial creates a focal point in the garden of a Long Island home.

PAGE 100: A Gingko chair by Claude Lalanne.

PAGE 168: An artisanal Wayuu *mochila* (bag) and a hand-woven Wayuu hat rest atop a faux tortoiseshell and ivory chest.

PAGE 230: An artwork by my wife, Marcia, rests on a shelf in the bedroom I created for a show house in Sag Harbor.

PAGE 271: A mood board of bead necklaces and amulets I've collected all over the world, all laid on an antique suzani.